Bonelli's eagle feather

Ruffed grouse feather

Common quail egg

House sparrow egg

Northern cardinal feather

Wedge-tailed eagle feather

Blue and yellow macaw feather

Peacock feather

Northern gannet feather

Domestic chicken down feather

Meadowlark egg

For Tharu, and every kid who is excited by the sound of the birds and the rush of the wind. Don't let big buildings stop you from experiencing the world's best playground among the trees.

– N.P

For Marc and Mel, who have accompanied me in the wonderful world of birds during our excursions through forests and mountains. And Bruna, because I hope to be able to teach and guide you in the spectacular and wild nature of this world.

– M.G

First published in Australia by Allen & Unwin in 2026, by arrangement with
Flying Eye Books Ltd., 27 Westgate Street, London, E8 3RL

Allen & Unwin
Cammeraygal Country
83 Alexander Street Crows Nest NSW 2065 Australia
Phone: (61 2) 8425 0100 Email: info@allenandunwin.com
Web: www.allenandunwin.com

*Allen & Unwin acknowledges the Traditional Owners of the Country on which we live and work.
We pay our respects to all Aboriginal and Torres Strait Islander Elders, past and present.*

A catalogue record for this book is available from the
National Library of Australia (catalogue.nla.gov.au)

ISBN 978 1 76118 289 1

For teaching resources, explore allenandunwin.com/learn

Design by Maisy Ruffels
Set in 11 pt Greycliff Gurmukhi

1 3 5 7 9 10 8 6 4 2

WHAT MAKES A BIRD?

An Illustrated Guide to the Bird World

Nadeem Perera
Montse Galbany

ALLEN&UNWIN
SYDNEY • MELBOURNE • AUCKLAND • LONDON

Contents

Introduction

In every climate, on every continent, birds abound. From thick rainforest canopies to city skyscrapers, birds have adapted to every habitat on Earth since the time of the dinosaurs. Some go on epic journeys while others stay in the same area their whole lives. There are those that weave nests, species that use their beaks as tools, and even birds with glow-in-the-dark night vision. Join us as we journey through the majestic, skilful, and surprising behaviours of the bird world.

What Makes a Bird?

All birds have wings (whether or not they can fly) and all birds have beaks, feathers, and two legs. But what else makes a bird?

The smallest bird in the world is the **Cuban bee hummingbird**, a mere 6.2 cm (2.5 inches) long. Its eggs are the size of coffee beans!

A Bird's Body

All birds have feathers, and they're the only animals that grow them. Their bodies have lots of other special features too...

Light bones

Birds don't have heavy bones. This makes it easier for them to move and fly around.

Bald eagle

Strength

Most birds can fly. They have strong muscles in their wings and chest that help them take off.

Feathers

Birds have feathers that help them stay warm, and in most cases, help them fly.

Laying eggs

Birds lay eggs, often in a nest, and baby birds grow inside them until they're ready to hatch.

Warm inside

Birds are warm-blooded like humans. They can stay at the same temperature in different weather.

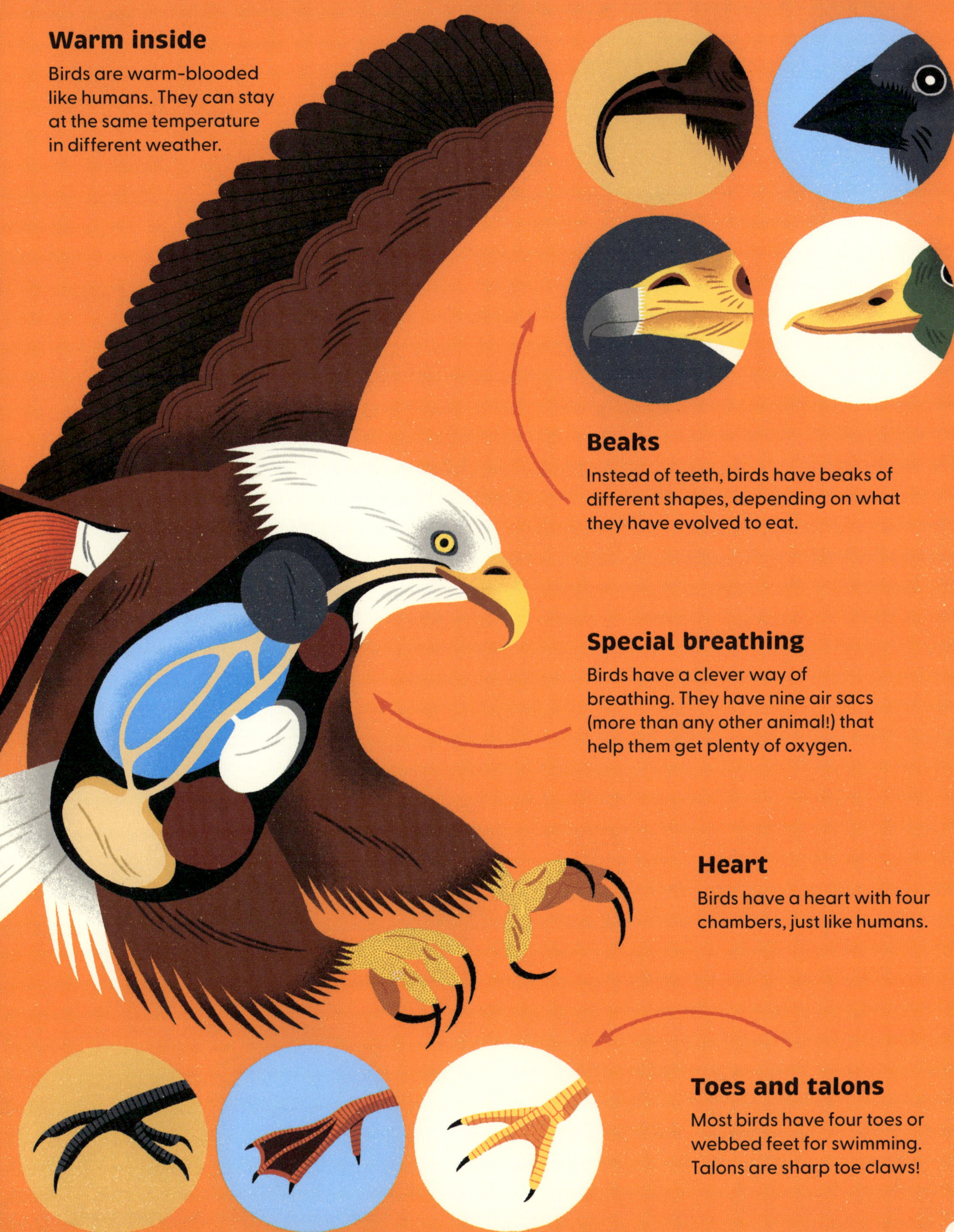

Beaks

Instead of teeth, birds have beaks of different shapes, depending on what they have evolved to eat.

Special breathing

Birds have a clever way of breathing. They have nine air sacs (more than any other animal!) that help them get plenty of oxygen.

Heart

Birds have a heart with four chambers, just like humans.

Toes and talons

Most birds have four toes or webbed feet for swimming. Talons are sharp toe claws!

Bird Evolution

When did birdlife begin? One of the first birds ever recorded by scientists lived during the time of dinosaurs, around 150 million years ago.

Many dinosaurs had feathers or hair all over their body. But only some dinosaurs had wings and could fly.

Being able to fly meant they could better find food and escape danger.

Dinosaur extinction

Flying probably saved birds from extinction 66 million years ago. All dinosaurs went extinct except feathered therapods, which eventually became the 10,000 species of birds we see today.

Ancient bird species

Some birds have hardly changed since prehistoric times, and have managed to avoid extinction over millions of years without having to completely evolve.

Having evolved 20 million years ago, **African ostriches** are one of the oldest living bird species. They have survived because they are big, strong, and speedy.

Ostriches are the largest birds on Earth. They have long, muscly legs perfect for sprinting to escape predators!

Take Flight

Birds have light bones full of space for air, which makes it easier for them to fly. Oxygen-rich blood flows through their bodies, giving them the energy for long flights.

Flying V

Canada geese fly together in a V-shape. Each bird flies a little above and behind the bird in front of them, which makes it easier and quicker to fly against the wind.

Head in the clouds

The **common swift** appears in Europe in the summer, after travelling more than 17,700 km (nearly 11,000 miles) from southern Africa. They spend more than 99% of the time in the air without needing to touch ground!

Flocking together

A group or gathering of birds is known as a 'flock'. There is safety in numbers, and synchronised flight formations make it easier for birds to travel longer distances.

Starlings fly in a 'murmuration' – a flock with as many as six million individuals! The birds gracefully dance across the sky together as one big mass, forming giant dotted patterns in the sky.

European starlings perform this mesmerising spectacle at dusk during autumn and winter.

Scientists aren't sure why starlings form murmurations, but the constant movement might be a way of confusing and throwing off predators.

Flightless Birds

Even though they all have feathers, not all birds fly. Flightless birds evolved to run or swim instead to suit their lifestyles.

Diving birds

Some birds, like penguins, have heavier bones to help them dive deep down under the water to catch their food.

Flightless birds

Some birds can't fly because they lack the right muscles in their chests, so they have other ways to hunt, travel, and escape predators.

Because Oceania separated from other continents so long ago, its animals evolved uniquely, and there aren't many predators. Therefore, instead of having to fly to flee from predators or find food, cassowaries grew large and strong.

Birdsong

Birds are admired for their chirpy singing all over the world. Have you ever wondered how, when, and why they make such beautiful sounds?

Dawn chorus

Birds sing just before or as the sun rises, in what's known as the 'dawn chorus'. Each bird has a set role and order, like a choir. If you wake up early you can hear it yourself!

Voice box

Humans have a larynx (voice box) with one air passage, while birds have two. This means they can make two sounds at once. That'd be like you speaking two sentences at the same time!

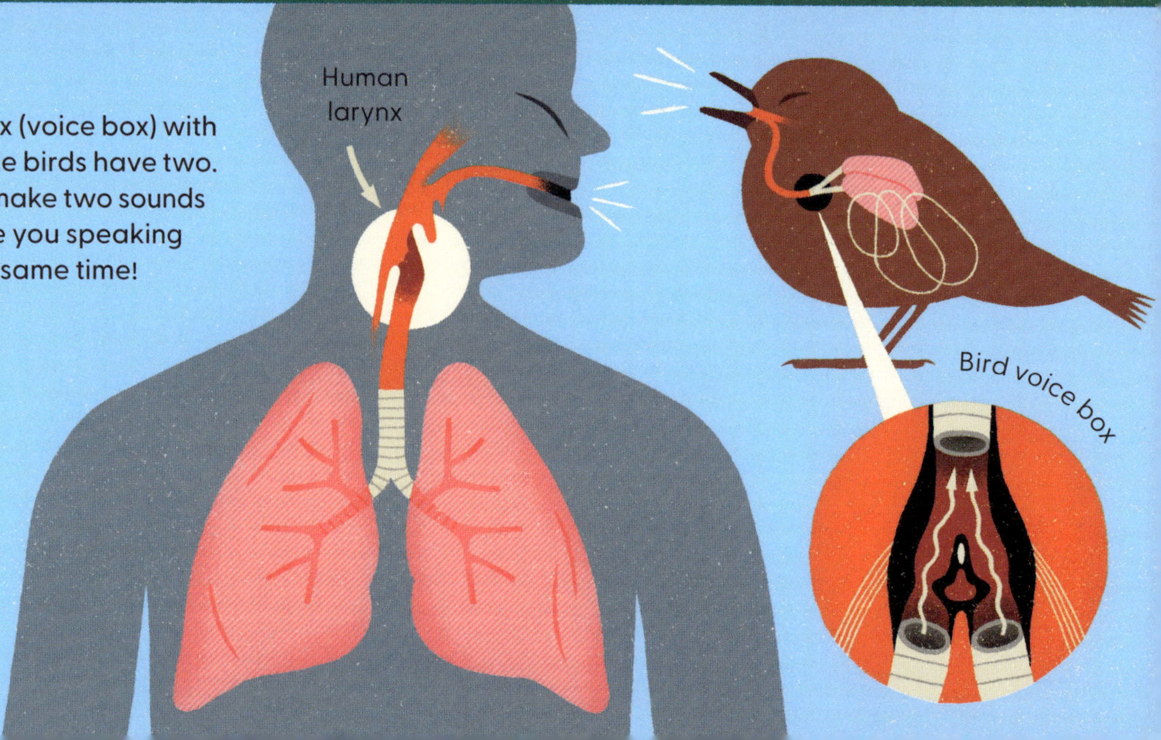

Passerine songbirds

Songbirds are also called 'passerines' and their beautiful tweets have inspired people for centuries.

The **skylark** prefers open grasslands for breeding seasons. This setting is ideal for its grand performances.

1. During the breeding season, skylarks bellow their song as loudly as possible.

2. They soar up to 200 metres (656 feet), singing to show off, claim territory, and attract a mate.

3. They descend after a few minutes, though some aerial displays can last up to half an hour!

Plumages

Every species of bird has feathers. They can be silky, fluffy, stripy, spotty, colourful, and cleverly camouflaged. There are wing, tail, and waterproof plumages – and ones just for showing off!

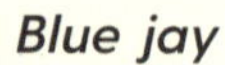

Blue jay

True blue

Blue birds aren't truly blue. Their feathers absorb all colours except blue, which scatters and is what we see. If you rotate a blue jay's feather, the blue may disappear, revealing dark brown feathers instead!

Gentoo penguin

Bird of many feathers

Penguins are a type of bird that swim instead of fly. Their short, waterproof feathers are tightly packed, to aid swimming and keep warm as they spend up to 75% of their time in cold water.

Courtship displays

In the bird world, looks really do matter! Many birds perform a feather display to attract a mate. The more extravagant the ritual, the more good-looking they seem.

The male Indian peafowl, a **peacock**, has one of the most impressive courtship displays. It raises its shimmering jewel-like feathers to dazzle a potential mate.

1 The peacock faces a peahen, lifts its 2-metre-long (6.56 feet) train and splays out its feathers to create a huge fan.

2 They give them a shake, creating a rustling sound and vibrating about 25 times per second! This is known as 'train-rattling'.

3 **Peahens** will decide to mate with the peacocks with the best feathers and displays. If a male's feathers look healthy and are still intact, it's a good sign that he hasn't run into much trouble.

FACT FILE

Feathers

Feathers help give some birds the ability to fly, but there is a lot more to them than catching wind. They help birds communicate, camouflage, keep them warm, and scare away predators.

The **Australian tawny frogmouth** is nocturnal, so it camouflages well in trees while sleeping during the day.

Some birds have clumps of feathers on their heads called 'crests', used to show when the bird is excited, threatened, or curious.

Sulphur-crested cockatoo

Owls have special feathers on their faces called 'bristle feathers' that help direct sound to their ears.

Short-eared owl

Cygnets (baby swans) hatch with grey feathers. They turn brown, then greyish, and finally white or black when fully grown.

There are birds that produce a waterproof oil that they apply to their feathers – using their beaks!

Mallard

Soft down feathers help keep baby birds warm by trapping air, but they can't be used to fly.

Turkey chick

Bird's Eye View

Bird vision is often 'overlooked'! But they have the largest eyes for their size of any animal besides frogs. Many birds have an excellent sense of smell and eyesight.

Golden eagle

Eagle Eyed

An eagle's vision is among the sharpest in the animal kingdom, allowing them to spot prey from 3.2 km (1.98 miles) away. Despite being smaller than humans, eagles' eyes are roughly the same size as ours!

All birds have a third eyelid. This helps protect them from sunlight, even while looking directly into the sun.

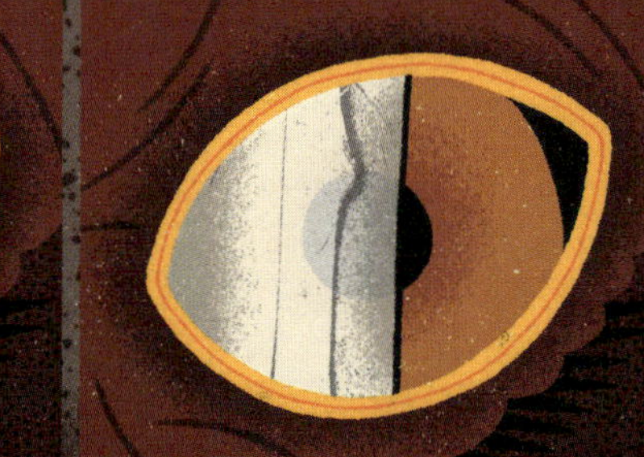

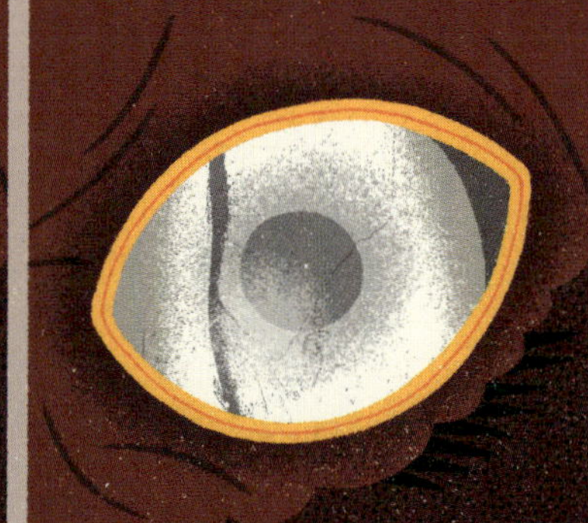

Night sight

UV (ultraviolet) light rays from the sun are invisible to humans, but visible to birds! About half of all bird species can see UV trails on nectar, trees, and plants, helping them find food.

The human eye has three cones for colour vision. Birds, like the **common kestrel**, have a fourth cone for seeing UV light.

Bird vision

Human vision

Common kestrels hover to find their prey.

Kestrels use their vision to spot urine trails from small mammals, which glow under UV light. They can follow these trails straight to their next meal!

Blue tit

African grey parrot

Australian magpie

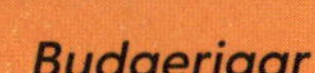

Budgerigar

FACT FILE

Eyes

What's it like to have a bird's eye view of the world? Here are some fascinating and surprising facts about avian eyesight.

Some birds, like nightjars, have oil droplets in their eyes that help them filter light so they can hunt at night.

Parrots are some of the only birds that sleep deeply like humans, which means they might have dreams!

Potoos have slits in their eyelids that allow them to detect movement even when their eyes are closed!

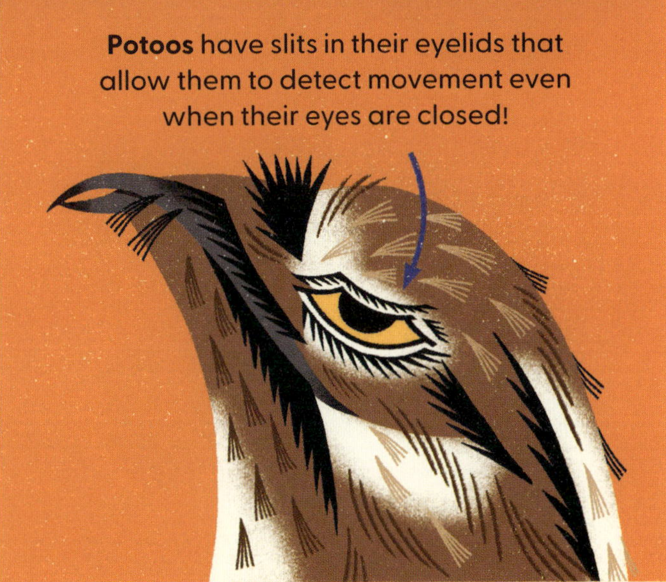

Hawks generally have eyes on the sides of their head, but can see forwards, too.

Beaks and Bills

A key feature of a bird is its beak, and many beaks are unique. Different types give us clues about each bird's behaviour, diet, and lifestyle.

Darwin's finches

On the Galápagos Islands, Charles Darwin discovered that finches of the same species had evolved different beaks to suit the food they ate on each island!

Sharp and soft

Waterbirds like ducks use their smooth, flat beaks and teeth filters to sift through water and mud to find little creatures to eat.

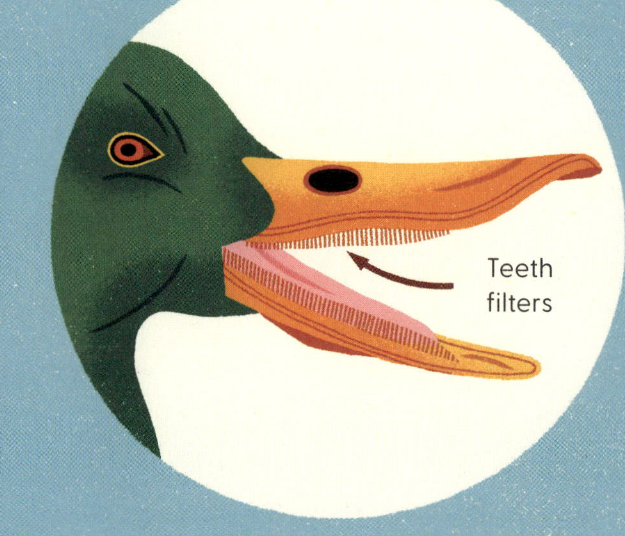

Unique beaks

Unusual or oversized beaks are often a sign of a bird's particular lifestyle and diet.

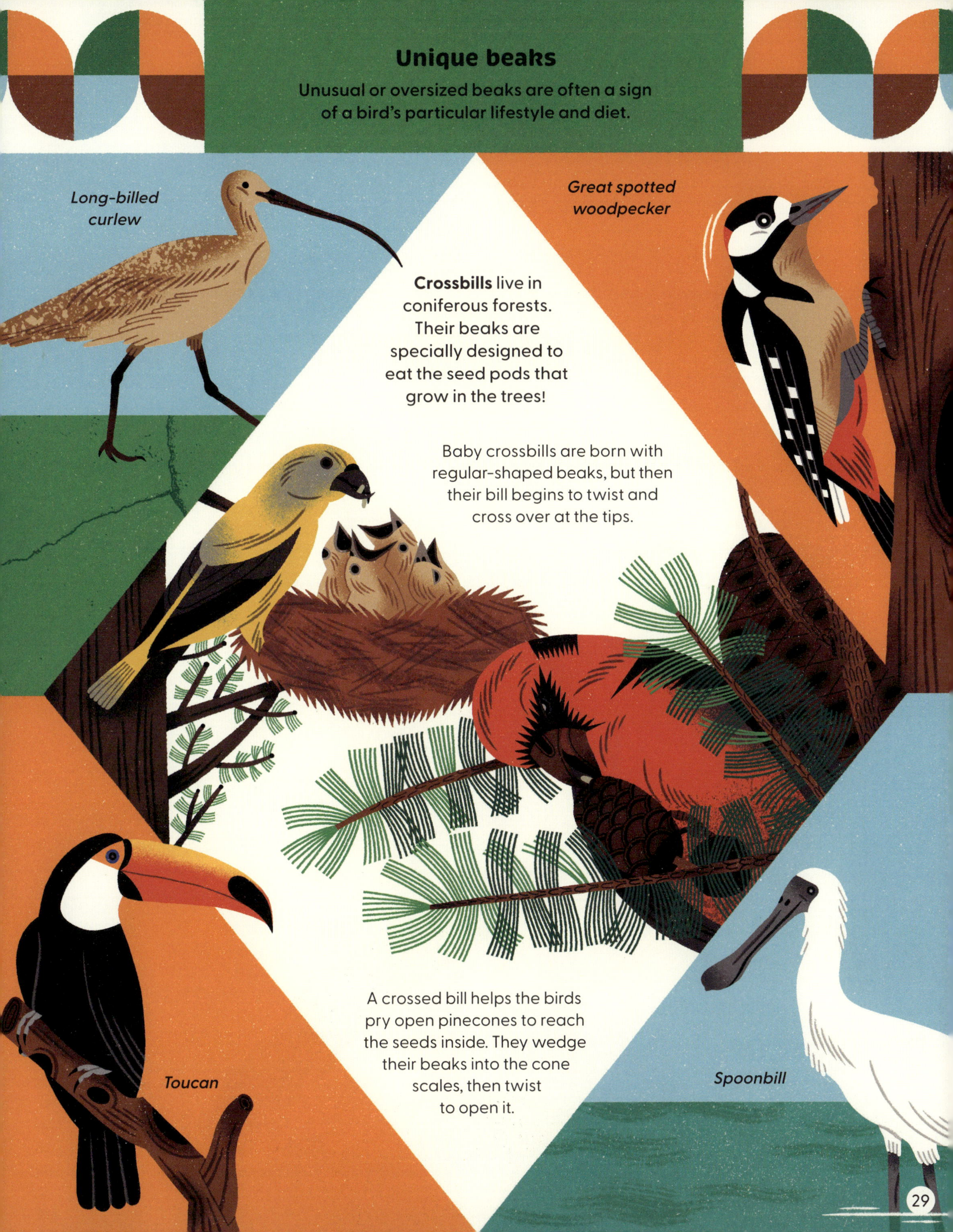

Crossbills live in coniferous forests. Their beaks are specially designed to eat the seed pods that grow in the trees!

Baby crossbills are born with regular-shaped beaks, but then their bill begins to twist and cross over at the tips.

A crossed bill helps the birds pry open pinecones to reach the seeds inside. They wedge their beaks into the cone scales, then twist to open it.

FACT FILE

Beaks

Beaks are an essential part of being a bird. From powerful dagger-like beaks to flat rounded spoons, to pin-like thin bills, each beak serves a purpose.

The outer layers of beaks are made of keratin (the same stuff as human nails) and can also grow back if damaged.

Bird beaks don't just include the bird's mouth but its nose, too!

Woodpeckers have strong, pointed chisel-like beaks for hammering holes into wood so they can reach food like tree sap or insects.

The edges of a toucan's huge beak are serrated like the blade of a knife. This tool helps them slice through rainforest fruits with hard skin.

Where Do Birds Live?

Different species of birds show that they handle whatever the planet throws at them. Penguins flourish in icy waters, wallcreepers conquer mountain faces, and pigeons colonise cities.

Great hornbills have a special way of nesting. Using dung and food, the male helps seal the female inside a tree, leaving a tiny eye hole. The female lays eggs inside while the male provides food deliveries!

Oceans

Ocean birds must be quick-thinking and fast-moving. Birds that brave the seas tackle strong winds, crashing waves, and big beasts.

Below

Most aquatic birds, like **gannets**, use their webbed feet as a rudder, to steer them in the right directions underwater. Bird swimming speeds need to match that of the fish they want to catch.

Above

Seabirds, like the **Manx shearwater**, are fast and have good eyesight so they can catch prey near the surface of the ever-moving current. They twist and turn in the air to avoid sharks and seals.

Albatrosses are masters of the seas. They are fantastic navigators, and can spend up to five years at sea, without visiting land. The wandering albatross has huge wings, 3.5 metres (11.4 feet) wide, that help it use the wind to glide over the open ocean.

Some birds such as fulmars, albatrosses, and petrels are called 'tubenoses' due to their tube-shaped nostrils which have a special filter that removes salt from seawater so that they can drink it.

King penguin

Birds that brave the deep have eyes that can see underwater. Below the waves, king penguins' pupils expand more than any other bird's to let in more light when they dive to dark depths of 300 metres (984 feet).

Mountains

Mountains can be harsh habitats for birds. They must brave high altitudes, rugged terrain, and scarce food. Against the odds, birds find ways to make unforgiving peaks work to their advantage.

Raven

Upper and lower middle

Corvids and **falcons** inhabit the upper middle; owls occupy the lower middle. They can be found at the base, but prefer the peace and quiet up here!

Himalayan bulbul

Grandala

Himalayan wood owl

Base

In the foothills of the Himalayas, you can spot the bright blue grandala, the bulbul, and the fluffy collared falconet.

Peak

There is less oxygen at the top. **Bearded vultures** can handle low air supplies, and eat what other birds consider 'waste'. Bones make up to 90% of their diet!

Wallcreepers are tiny birds that live in crevices in mountain faces. They use their long beaks to find insects scuttling within the rocks.

Golden eagles are the most dominant mountain birds. In Mongolia, Kazakh eagle hunters have used them to hunt prey during winter for centuries.

Woodland

When you think of where birds live, woodlands are the most obvious habitat. But lots of other animals also live in trees, so birds must compete for food, shelter, and territory.

Treetops and skies

Birds of prey, such as buzzards, **goshawks**, and **kites**, can be seen soaring above woodlands. They use forests for nesting but hunt far and wide.

Tree trunks

Tree-dwelling birds like chickadees, **treecreepers**, waxwings, and **great spotted woodpeckers** rely on berries, insect larvae, and tree holes for survival. Their small size helps them thrive above the leaf litter.

Forest floor

Brave birds such as wrens, **blackbirds**, American robins, and green woodpeckers risk running into residents such as foxes, wildcats, and snakes. Fallen leaves and fungi are used to build nests, while insects make the perfect meal.

Woodpeckers drill holes in trees to make nests that predators cannot easily get to, or to find larvae that is hidden beneath the tree bark.

Goshawks and other forest raptors have wide, short wings that make them nimble for moving between trees.

Deserts

Deserts are tough places to live, with scorching hot temperatures and little water to drink or plants to eat. Birds here must find clever ways to survive.

Shrubland and desert flats

Roadrunners and hummingbirds live among trees in North American deserts. Hummingbirds feed on insects, nectar, and cactus fruit such as prickly pears. Roadrunners eat lizards and snakes.

Steppe

Mongolian ground jays and hoopoes live in the dry, grassy plains and forests, known as steppes, of the large, cold Gobi Desert in Mongolia and China.

Mountains and rocky plateaus

Desert vultures have evolved to 'scavenge', feed, on dead animals. This might seem gross, but getting rid of decaying flesh helps prevent disease from spreading through the desert.

The **Rüppell's vulture**, of sub-Saharan Africa, is the highest-flying bird. It soars up to 11,000 metres (36,089 feet) high. That's roughly 30 Empire State buildings! Up here, it can scan for food.

Owls don't only live in the woods. Tiny **burrowing owls** live in underground dens to keep safe and cool in North and South American deserts.

Polar Regions

The North and South poles see constant daylight in summer and no sunrise in winter. Their birds must cope with snow, ice, strong wings, and freezing climates. So how do they survive?

Sea ice Antarctic

Penguins and **snow petrels** live in Antarctica. Penguins are the only birds that breed on sea ice, using it to slide into the ocean for food. Snow petrels perch on icebergs and islands, where they create nests made from pebbles.

Tundra Arctic

Though the **Arctic redpoll** is miniature in size and weighs less than a chocolate bar, it can endure Arctic tundra temperatures as low as -50°C (58°F).

Sea cliffs Antarctic

Birds such as the **Antarctic shag** nest in big sea cliff colonies in the Southern Ocean off the coast of Antarctica. They dive from the water surface to catch krill and squid.

Water Arctic

Nicknamed 'sea parrots', puffins spend most of their lives in the open ocean, paddling, resting, swimming, or diving.

Atlantic puffin

Cities

In cities, skyscrapers replace cliffs, trains criss-cross the ground, and millions of people live in small spaces. Most urban jungles are home to birds, but there is always more we can do to make them welcome.

Magnificent frigatebird

Rio de Janeiro, Brazil

Many of Rio's birds are as colourful as the city's famous Carnival. You can spot toco toucans and bright yellow saffron finches along with magnificent frigatebirds with their bright red chests.

New York, USA

Pockets of green spaces can serve as a great habitat for wildlife in cities. Pigeons, cardinals, and the American robin flourish in New York's Central Park – they just have to avoid the red-tailed hawk!

London, UK

London is home to over 10 million people and 400 species of bird. Among them, the **ring-necked parakeet** – originally from South Asia – has learned to thrive, despite no one truly knowing how they got here!

Akita, Japan

Crows are highly intelligent, especially with tools and problem-solving. In Akita, they have been seen to drop walnuts onto roads so cars drive over them and crack the shells, allowing the crows to swoop in and eat the nuts!

Tokyo, Japan

Only 8% of Tokyo is green space, but still there are over 700 species of bird living in the city. Japanese white-eyes and kingfishers can be seen flitting about the busiest city in the world.

Sydney, Australia

In Sydney you can hear the laugh of the kookaburra, see pelicans resting on lampposts, and spot flocks of rainbow lorikeets splashing colour across the sky.

Pigeons are the most common city bird. They live in groups, which protects them against predators. They are descended from **rock doves** who live on clifftops. This means pigeons feel right at home atop skyscrapers!

Flocks of pigeons attract hungry falcons. **Peregrine falcons** have adapted especially well to life in cities around the world.

Rainforests

The world's dense, lush rainforests lie near the equator. Flashes of colourful plumages dart by every minute, and treetop canopies ring with melodic calls. Birds are kept busy hunting, pollinating plants, and munching on fruit and insects.

Scarlet macaw

Canopy

The canopy is a lively hub where most animals in the rainforest live. Parrots, jacamars, and many more birds inhabit this tier.

Blue-throated barbet

Understory

This understory is filled with shrubs and young trees that compete for sunlight in the shade of towering giants. Trogons and barbets fly very little, nesting in tree holes and feasting on insects and lizards.

Malayan peacock-pheasant

Forest floor

It's much darker on the forest floor than in the upper rainforest levels, so fewer plants grow. Birds such as the Malayan peacock-pheasant in Southeast Asia and the magnificent riflebird in Australia and New Guinea forage for seeds, fruits, and insects.

Emergent layer

This is the highest level of trees. Flying up here in the Amazon rainforest is the **harpy eagle**, believed to be the most powerful bird on earth. Its huge talons can even crush monkeys and sloths.

Rufous-tailed jacamar

Bare-cheeked trogon

Magnificent riflebird

Myna birds hitch rides on elephants' backs, feeding on bugs that jump out when the elephant uproots plants. In return, the birds remove ticks and parasites from the elephant.

Mohican-haired turacos, found in dense African rainforests, are known for their bright green colour. They are the only bird with a truly green pigment in their feathers.

The **red junglefowl**, found in South and Southeast Asia, is the ancestor of domesticated chickens, which means that chickens surprisingly come from the rainforest!

What Do Birds Do?

Birds have different lifestyles. Social flamingos live in flocks, while kingfishers are solitary birds. Some birds migrate over long distances, while others stay in the same area year-round.

Andean flamingo

Flamingos flock together in their hundreds and even thousands. By lakes, lagoons and swamps, feeding on things like shrimp – which turns their feathers pink. A group is known as a 'flamboyance of flamingos'!

Coupling Up

Around 90% of birds are socially monogamous – this means they have one mate at a time. Having two parents able to incubate the eggs and search for food helps the baby birds reach adulthood.

Laysan albatross

Enduring love

Albatrosses are true romantics, often forming bonds for life. Couples endure long separations when travelling huge distances across oceans, but they faithfully reunite at breeding grounds.

Lifelong bonds

Birds have fascinating love stories. Some birds pair up for life, finding remarkable ways to navigate it together.

Killer Strategies

Given that birds come from dinosaurs, it's no surprise that many are brilliant hunters. There are lots of different tricks that birds employ to catch their dinner.

Herons

Herons are patient hunters. They can stand as still as a statue for hours waiting to strike, before jabbing a spear-like beak into fish in rivers and streams.

Grey heron

Little impaler

Nicknamed 'the butcherbird', shrikes are small but brutal. They skewer insects, small rodents, and small birds on thorns...ouch!

Shrike

Birds of prey

This term describes many different bird families, together known as raptors. Raptors include eagles, hawks, falcons, vultures and more!

The fastest-known animal in the entire world is the **peregrine falcon**. It can fly up to speeds of 390 kph! It is so successful at hunting that it's adapted to living in almost every type of habitat.

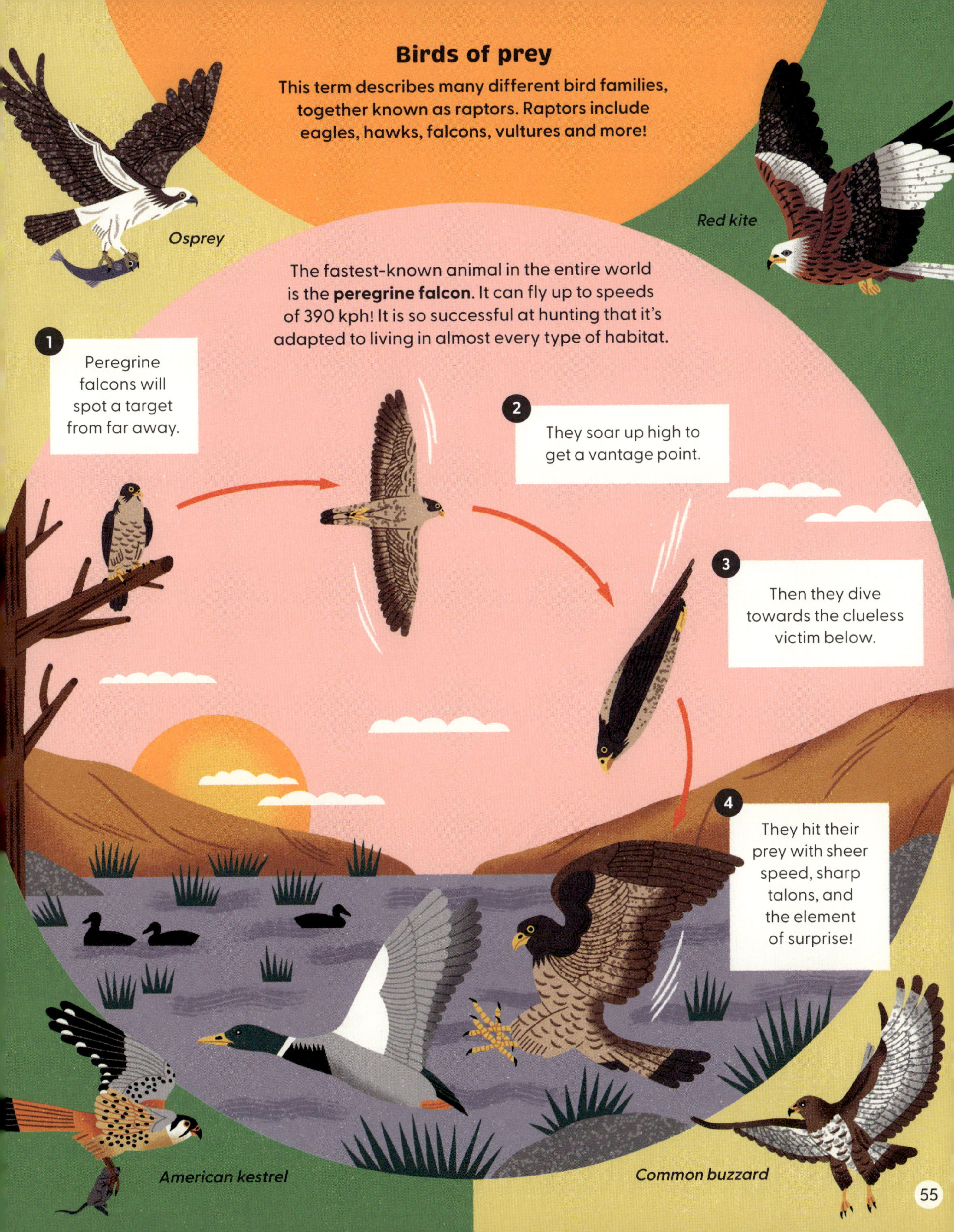

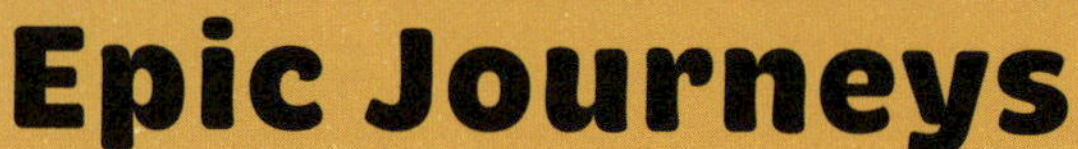

Epic Journeys

Migration is one of the wonders of the bird world: just how do they know where to go? Notice the birds around you – they may be visitors from the other side of the world!

Longest journey

The **Arctic tern** has the longest bird migration. They travel over 88,500 km (55,000 miles) from the North Pole to the South Pole every year, and can even eat and sleep while flying!

Hollow bones

The wandering bird

The biggest flying bird is the **wandering albatross**. It can travel over oceans as far as the distance between London and Sydney.

Long-distance migrations

From the Arctic to the tropics, these feathered globetrotters go on epic adventures over tens of thousands of miles.

In 2022, a tiny five-month-old **bar-tailed godwit** set the world record for the longest non-stop bird migration of 13,560 km (8,425 miles). This journey took 11 days and one hour, from Alaska to Tasmania.

FACT FILE

Navigation

Around 50% of birds migrate. Seabirds, songbirds, and raptors share flyways across the world, going north to south and back again.

Bar-headed geese can reach heights of 8 km (4.97 miles) above sea level when migrating over the world's tallest mountains, the Himalayas.

Homing pigeons are known for using impeccable navigation skills to find their way back home. During the First and Second World Wars, they delivered important letters that were tied to their legs.

Warblers, along with other songbirds, opt for night-time migrations, as there is less risk of being dehydrated from the Sun's heat.

White storks have formed lifelong bonds with humans in countries such as Türkiye and Serbia, returning yearly to nest in the same chimneys and gardens.

Thanks to bird feeders in UK gardens, some populations of blackcap now migrate from Europe to the UK for the winter!

Eurasian blackcap warbler

Nesting

From master weavers to mud architects, birds have invented practical, genius, and strange methods for building homes to raise the next generation.

Supersized structures

The world's largest nest belongs to the **sociable weaver**, which can be up to six metres (19 feet) wide! Made with twigs and dry grasses, they form a thatched roof and dozens of chambers. These mansions can remain in use for over a century, housing up to 400 birds at one time. A social crowd, indeed!

Stitched up

The **common tailorbird** of Asia's tropics is an incredible nest-builder. The talented female punctures holes in leaves with her sharp beak, then uses plant fibres (similar to cotton) and spiderwebs to 'sew' the edges together, even knotting them in place. The result is a snug cradle for her young.

Unusual roosts

Birds can, and do, make themselves right at home in the most unexpected places.

Edible-nest swiftlets are small birds found in Southeast Asia, who have a peculiar talent of building nests made almost entirely of their own saliva!

The birds build these nests in secluded, damp, dark spaces – from caves to clifftops. Their saliva hardens and sticks to the rocky walls, like drool cement. Pretty gross!

Some nests are farmed to make a highly prized and extremely expensive dish: bird's nest soup.

FACT FILE

Nests

Birds build nests to raise young, and so they have to be as safe, camouflaged, and sheltered as possible – all tough things to achieve in the unpredictable natural world.

Redstart

Cuckoos have found a sneaky way to get free babysitters. They lay their eggs in another bird's nest, tricking them into raising the chicks as their own!

Young cuckoo

Cuckoo's egg

Kingfishers dig their own nest tunnels, sometimes structuring them with regurgitated fish bones!

European bee-eaters excavate burrows in the sides of riverbanks, returning to nest after catching insects in flight.

Peregrine numbers are on the up in cities such as London and New York, as skyscrapers and bridges have become their adopted homes.

Coots nest on anything they can find along rivers and canals – from narrowboats to floating buoys.

Nature's Gardeners

Birds help shape the natural world by pollinating plants and spreading seeds. When they feed, they carry seeds and pollen as they flit away, helping new plants grow.

Fruit farmers

There are over 50 kinds of fruit doves, and they love eating fruit! By dropping seeds (in their poo!), they help grow new trees and keep forests healthy.

Flower power

Some birds have a sweet tooth! They use their tiny, curved beaks to sip the sweet nectar from a flower, before zipping off to find more treats.

Hummingbirds beat their wings about 80 times per second and have hearts that pump 1,200 times per minute! This helps them to hover and feed as often as possible on their favourite food – nectar from flowers.

Because of how much energy they need for flying, hummingbirds can travel up to 40 km (24.85 miles) in a day, moving from flower to flower.

Hummingbirds love bright pink and red flowers, especially ones with tubes holding lots of tasty nectar, like trumpet creepers.

The **Anna's hummingbird** is common along America's west coast. It thrives living alongside humans.

Night Vision

Nocturnal birds rule the realms of the dark night until sunrise. Their night vision and excellent hearing make this the ideal time for them to hunt.

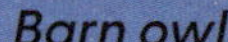

Barn owl

Masters of the night

Owls have big, powerful eyes. If owls were human-sized, their eyes would be the size of grapefruits! They see well at night due to reflective layers in their eyes, and are experts at spotting movement in the dark.

Echolocation

Echolocation is letting out lots of 'clicking' sounds and working out how long it takes for the sound to bounce back to the ear to tell how far away it is. The only birds with this ability are oilbirds and swiftlets.

The faster the sound comes back, the closer whatever you're flying into is, like an internal map system for when the sun goes down!

The **South American oilbird** uses echolation in the dark caves they nest in.

Becoming a Birder

Birding, or birdwatching, is easier than you might think. With the right steps, you can spot, identify, and help care for the birds around you.

My birding journey: Nadeem

When I started birding, I had no idea what to look out for. I hadn't studied birds, and most of the time I wouldn't know what species I was looking at. So if you want to get into birding, but you don't know about all the birds we've looked at in this book, I'm here to tell you not to worry!

Where to start

1. Look outside

Even if you live in a bustling city or a high-rise building, you can spot birds. The first thing to do is to get outside or look out from your window, which can be a great vantage point!

2. Focus on the present

You might miss seeing a beautiful bird flit past if you are on your phone, or miss hearing a tuneful birdsong if you've got headphones on. It can be tough to be totally present in a busy world, but it gets easier with practice!

3. Look up

At trees, rooftops, fences, telephone wires, lampposts, in bushes or ponds: anywhere a bird might perch or paddle. Birding isn't about being in the countryside or being an expert, it's about connecting to the world around you.

Identify a Bird

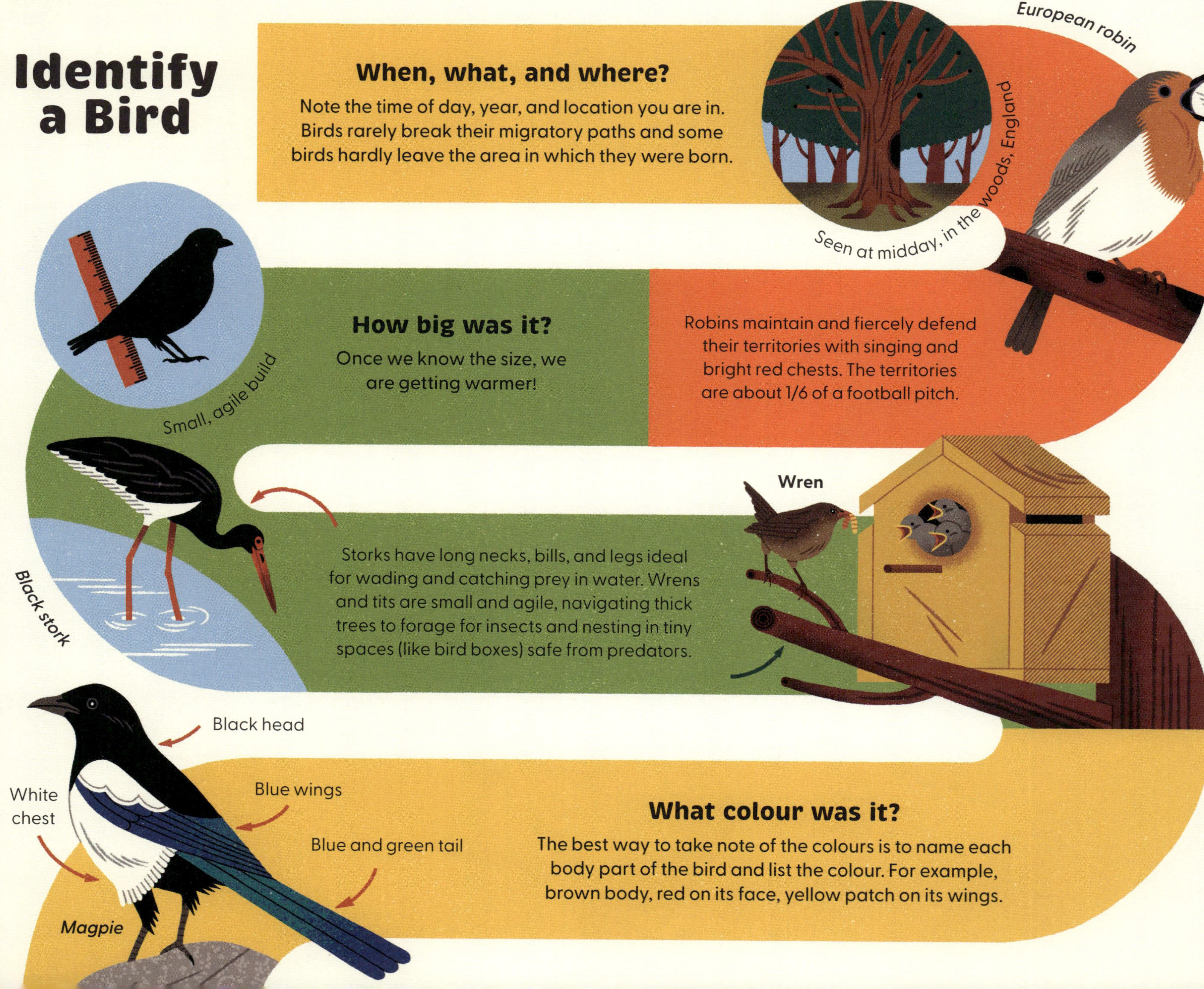

When, what, and where?

Note the time of day, year, and location you are in. Birds rarely break their migratory paths and some birds hardly leave the area in which they were born.

Robins maintain and fiercely defend their territories with singing and bright red chests. The territories are about 1/6 of a football pitch.

How big was it?

Once we know the size, we are getting warmer!

Storks have long necks, bills, and legs ideal for wading and catching prey in water. Wrens and tits are small and agile, navigating thick trees to forage for insects and nesting in tiny spaces (like bird boxes) safe from predators.

What colour was it?

The best way to take note of the colours is to name each body part of the bird and list the colour. For example, brown body, red on its face, yellow patch on its wings.

Female mandarin duck
Male mandarin duck
Often, males have more colourful a plumage used to attract mates, while females are more camouflage, which helps when nesting and looking after young.
Cheerful, fast-paced twittering melody
What was it doing?
This question will really help to whittle down the species. Bird behaviour tends to suit the environment they live in.
What kind of sound did it make?
Did it make a warbling sound, a high-pitched trill, or a raspy caw? Is it the same melody repeated, or is it a short burst of sound?
Twists and turns when in flight
Kestrels hover by facing the wind, adjusting their wings and tails to stay in place. In a breeze, they seem still, but on calm days, they flap faster. This helps them carefully scan the ground to spot scurrying rodents.
Now you have all the information you need to make an entry in your bird log!
A European goldfinch
So what was our bird?

Make a Bird Log

Make your own bird log! Keep a notebook or some paper near your favourite birdwatching spot and note down any details when you spot one. Logging these details will help you learn more about the birds when you get a chance to research them!

Step 1: Time and place

Note the time and location of the sighting. Is the bird most active in the morning? It is going back and forth feeding its young in a tree cavity? Like us, birds are active at different times and have habitat likes and dislikes.

Step 2: Size

Start by noting physical details. If a golden eagle is large and a robin is small, how big is the bird you've just seen? Small? Medium? Small-medium?

Step 3: Plumage

Are the head feathers a different colour to its body? Are its chest feathers patterned? Are its feathers soft or with a metallic sheen? Note the colour, patterns, and textures of the bird's feathers.

Step 4: Sounds

Write down the kind of chirp, whistle, shriek or hoot you can hear. Is it the same melody repeated, or is it a short burst of sound?

Step 5: Bird behaviour

Did the bird fly, feed, or hop about? Did it swoop, hover or twist and turn in the air? If it was eating, what was it – seeds, fruit, or scavenging? Was it alone or with a group of other birds – if so, how many?

Step 6: Research

Use a search engine, library, or bird book to research. For example, you could search 'small brown bird in North America with an orange chest'.

Take it further

You could get some binoculars and a pocket-sized guidebook, and ask an adult to download a free bird identifier app. You can join birding communities online or in person, and check out resources at the British Trust for Ornithology, RSPB, Audubon, BirdLife International, and the Great Backyard Bird Count.

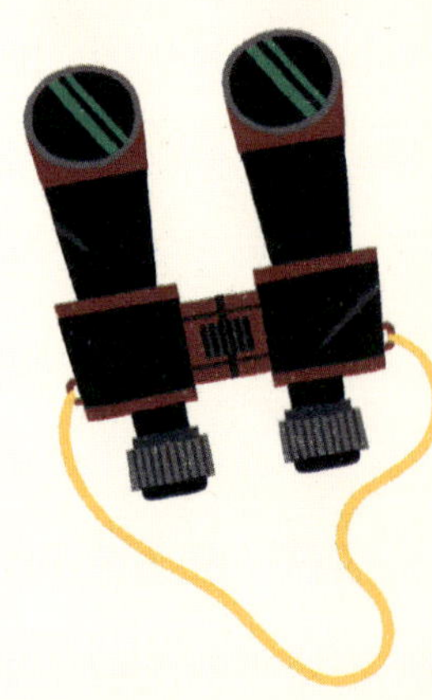

Birdwatching Logbook

Bird species

Date: 2/4/25 **Time:** 3.30pm

Season: ◯ Winter ◯ Spring ◯ Summer ◯ Autumn

Location: Where did you see them?

Size:

Small ◯ ◯ ◯ ◯ ◯ Large

Plumage: What do they look like?

Colour:

Chest

Wings

Head

Sound:

◯ Chirp ◯ Whistle ◯ Shriek ◯ Hoot ◯ Melody ◯ Repeated ◯ Single burst

Behaviour: What are they doing?

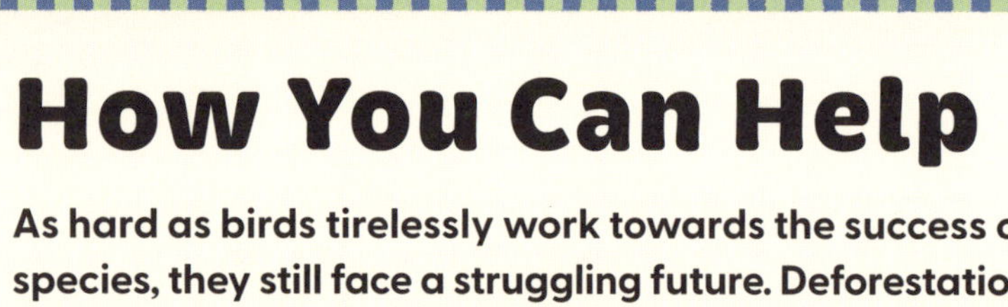

How You Can Help

As hard as birds tirelessly work towards the success of their species, they still face a struggling future. Deforestation, pollution, and climate change are threats to our feathered friends, but the good news is that small, everyday actions can go a long way.

Food and water

The easiest way to help birds is to provide food and water. You can make bird feeders and baths from recycled materials like plastic bottles and cups. There are also feeders that stick to your window! Remember to clean and move bird feeders to help stop the spread of diseases.

Plant life

Things that attract birds include insects, trees, and bushes filled with seeds and berries, and wildflowers and nectar-rich flowers. If you have outdoor space, you could install a bird box for nesting and a bird bath for resting and drinking.

Community

You could raise awareness and share your love of birds by starting a birdwatching club. I did this with a friend, and now we have a large group, TV show, and books dedicated to birds! A community fosters friendship, idea-sharing, and outdoor exploration, all priceless in today's fast-paced world.

How many ideas can you come up with to connect people with birds and the natural world? Everyone has the power to help make a real difference, in your garden, local community, country, and beyond!

Glossary

Adaptation – When a species evolves special features to improve its chances of survival

Aerodynamic – Evolved to move smoothly through the air with little resistance

Apex predator – Animals at the top of the food chain

Breeding ground – An environment where animals reproduce

Camouflage – An animal's appearance allowing them to blend in with their surroundings

Deforestation – The cutting down of large areas of trees

Ecosystem – The interaction between a community of living things and their environment

Extinction – When an entire species, or type, dies out

Fossils – The remains or traces of plants and animals that lived long ago

Habitat – A natural home for a living creature

Lagoon – A big, shallow pool of water separated from a larger body of water by land or coral reefs

Magnetic field – An invisible force created by forces inside of the earth

Migration – The movement of living things from one region to another, usually to find food, mates or warmer weather

Nocturnal – A creature that is most active at night and usually sleeps during the day

Permafrost – Ground that stays totally frozen for at least two years, typically near the Earth's North and South poles

Pollen – A substance produced by plants, allowing them to reproduce

Pollination – When pollen is transferred to the stigma of a flower by a pollinator (such as an insect or bird), the flower can be fertilised and turn into a fruit containing seeds

Pollution – Substances in the environment that can be harmful to living things. If something has too much pollution in it, it is called 'polluted'

Synchronised – Happening or moving together at the same time

Territory – The area an animal lives in, which they may defend from other animals

Therapod – Dinosaurs that walked on two legs, mostly carnivorous like *Tyrannosaurus rex* and *Velociraptor*

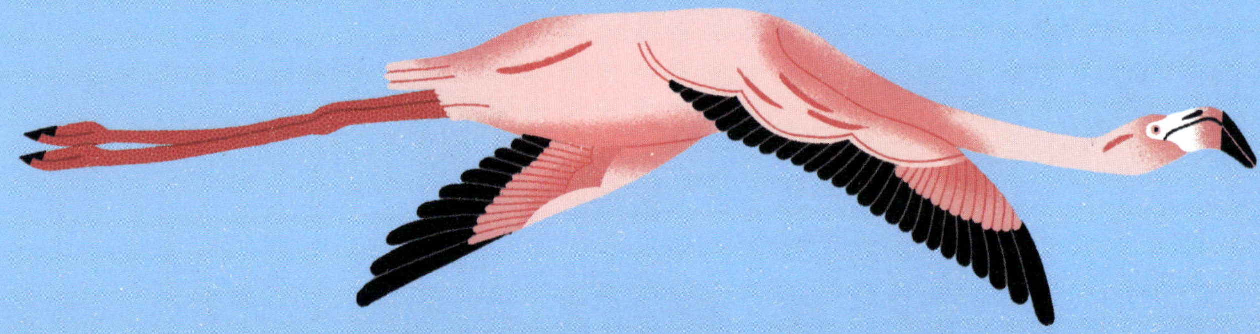

Bird Species Index

Written by Nadeem Perera

Nadeem Perera is a wildlife TV presenter, author, and activist. He is the co-founder of the birdwatching collective Flock Together, which encourages people of colour to get out, enjoy nature, and support each other. Born and raised in London, Nadeem's love of nature expressed itself at an early age when it helped him to overcome mental roadblocks and trauma. He has appeared on television shows such as *Springwatch*, *Winterwatch, The One Show,* and *One Zoo Three: Goes Wild in Britain.*

Illustrated by Montse Galbany

Montse Galbany started drawing as soon as she could hold a pencil and has never stopped since. She is an illustrator and graphic designer living in Granollers, a city close to Barcelona, Spain. She studied graphic design at Elisava University and has been working as an illustrator since 2017. She works digitally with friendly shapes and vibrant colours to tell stories. She has been published by Rebel Girls, Penguin Random House, and Editorial Planeta, among others.